THE LIBRARY OF
AMERICAN
LIVES AND TIMES™

WILLIAM TECUMSEH SHERMAN

The Fight to Preserve the Union

Lynn Hoogenboom

The Rosen Publishing Group's
PowerPlus Books™
New York

For my parents

Published in 2004 by The Rosen Publishing Group, Inc.
29 East 21st Street, New York, NY 10010

First Edition

Editor's Note: All quotations have been reproduced as they appeared in the letters and diaries from which they were borrowed. No correction was made to the inconsistent spelling that was common in that time period.

Library of Congress Cataloging-in-Publication Data

Hoogenboom, Lynn.
William Tecumseh Sherman : the fight to preserve the Union / Lynn Hoogenboom.— 1st ed.
   v. cm.— (The library of American lives and times)
Contents: A man of contradictions—Childhood and West Point—Missing the Mexican War—Leaving the army—A disastrous year—Grant shows the way—Triumph and tragedy—The Atlanta campaign—Sherman's marches—Commander of the army.
ISBN 0-8239-6625-9 (library binding)
1. Sherman, William T. (William Tecumseh), 1820–1891—Juvenile literature. 2. Generals—United States—Biography—Juvenile literature. 3. United States. Army—Biography—Juvenile literature. 4. United States—History—Civil War, 1861–1865—Campaigns—Juvenile literature. [1. Sherman, William T. (William Tecumseh), 1820–1891. 2. Generals. 3. United States—History—Civil War, 1861–1865. 4. Sherman's March to the Sea.] I. Title. II. Series.
  E467.1.S55 H66 2004
  355'.0092—dc21

                                                      2002009508

Manufactured in the United States of America

CONTENTS

1. A Man of Contradictions

The Civil War has been over for more than a century. Even so, the name William Tecumseh Sherman can still start an argument.

Although Sherman is considered by many to be the most brutal of all Civil War generals, he may have been responsible for fewer deaths than any other important general in the entire Civil War. He is still despised by some in the South, but he loved the South and considered himself its friend.

Sherman's critics point out that he never won a major battle. His admirers point out that he never lost a campaign. Before the war a military man would have told you that many of the feats that his troops would accomplish were impossible. He is both credited with and blamed for changing the way war is fought. Sherman probably would have told you that the Civil War itself changed the nature of war. He merely reacted to the changes.

Opposite: This photograph of William Tecumseh Sherman was taken around 1863. At West Point, Sherman studied the philosopher James Kent, who wrote that in civil war "the central government had to defend the laws of union by force of arms or be disgraced."

When the Civil War began, both the North and the South were sure that they would win the war quickly and easily. Both were convinced that their side was fighting for liberty. The South fought to protect the liberties of each state and to defend those liberties from the interference of the federal government. The North fought to save the Union, which protected individual liberties through the Bill of Rights. Later the war turned into a crusade to abolish slavery.

The Civil War was more deadly than any American war that had ever been fought before it. Guns were more accurate and easier to load, but the tactics most officers used at the beginning of the war were designed for inaccurate guns and bayonets. Military moves that had made sense when bullets rarely hit their targets could be disastrous when most of the bullets went where guns were aimed. Although casualties in places such as Shiloh, Antietam, Vicksburg, and Gettysburg mounted beyond anything anyone could have imagined, neither side was willing to give up.

It wasn't just a war of soldiers. The people at home also refused to give up. Citizens pitched in by wrapping bandages, working as hospital volunteers, and keeping farms and factories going.

When the war began, neither side was willing to admit that it was a war over slavery. It is impossible, however, to imagine the war taking place if slavery, a system in which one person could own another, had never existed.

In America, slavery also involved race. Slave owners were white, and slaves were black. Enslaved Africans had been forced onto ships in Africa and had been brought to America, where, if they survived the journey, they were sold at an auction to whoever offered the most money.

Slavery had never existed in Ohio, Sherman's birthplace, because it had been forbidden in the lands of the Northwest Territory by the Northwest Ordinance, a law that was passed in 1787. Many Americans hoped that slavery would gradually be abolished in the new United States, and that this law was a step toward seeing that happen. Eli Whitney's cotton gin and his development of interchangeable parts played a major role in ending these hopes.

The cotton gin, invented in 1793, made it extremely profitable for the South to grow cotton on plantations with slave labor. The cotton gin easily separated cotton from its seeds, a task that had previously been costly and time-consuming. Instead of feeling embarrassed about slavery, Southerners began to defend it as an economic necessity. Another Whitney innovation, making products with interchangeable parts, was developed between 1801 and 1807. This method of production helped manufacturing to grow in the Northeast. Having interchangeable parts meant that products such as guns could be produced quicker and at a lower cost. Because all parts were standardized, if a piece of a gun broke, it could be

This painting, believed to show the Shawnee chief Tecumseh, was given to the Chicago Natural History Museum in 1894. Tecumseh is depicted in the dress of a white man. Tecumseh was a charismatic leader and warrior whose name meant "celestial panther" or "shooting star."

replaced. In the past, one had to replace the whole gun. This innovation helped to turn the Northeast into an industrial powerhouse with needs that were completely different from the needs of the cotton-growing South.

Finally, the defeat of the brilliant Shawnee chief Tecumseh during the War of 1812 removed the last strong Native American barrier to westward expansion. The opening of the West created constant problems between the North and the South as new states sought to enter the Union as either slave or free states.

Tecumseh had managed to form a huge Indian confederation, or alliance, that stretched from the Great Lakes to the Gulf of Mexico. He told the Indian nations that if they stuck together, they could keep the settlers from taking over more Indian land. He favored peaceful methods over force and tried to end the brutality that had marked the battles between settlers and Indians.

Chief Tecumseh was also a talented warrior, and in the War of 1812 his forces fought for the British, who had guaranteed the Indians' landholdings. He was killed in Canada in the Battle of the Thames on October 5, 1813, when his Indian forces were far outnumbered by the American army.

Most northwesterners felt relieved when they heard of his death. Among those who felt regret was a lawyer in Lancaster, Ohio, named Charles Sherman. He decided that he would name one of his sons Tecumseh.

2. Childhood and West Point

Years passed before Charles Sherman was able to name a son Tecumseh. His first son was named for Charles's father. Charles's wife, Mary, insisted that their second son be named for her brother. Next two daughters were born. Finally, on February 8, 1820, another son was born. This child was named Tecumseh. His brothers and sisters called the new baby Cump. He was the sixth child in a family that would eventually number eleven children.

The Sherman children didn't know it, but their father had serious financial problems. When he first came to Lancaster, Ohio, from Connecticut, Charles Sherman was one of Ohio's tax collectors. In those days, most of the money in Ohio was printed and issued by local banks. In 1816, the government decided that too much paper money was being used, and it announced that it would only accept money issued by the United States Bank. The money that Charles Sherman's deputies had already collected was worth nothing, and Charles Sherman owed the government that entire amount in United States Bank money.

Charles Sherman spent the rest of his life paying off the debt. He continued to do well as a lawyer, though, and in 1823, he became an Ohio Supreme Court judge. During most of the year, Charles traveled from town to town, judging cases.

Cump was born in this house on Main Street in Lancaster, Ohio. The Victorian brick front was added in 1870. Near the time of Sherman's birth in 1820, stagecoaches began making regular stops in Lancaster.

When Cump was nine, tragedy struck his family. While Charles Sherman was traveling, he suddenly became ill. Cump's mother quickly left to join him. Before she reached him, however, she received word that it was too late. Charles Sherman had died.

Because all Charles Sherman's extra money had gone to pay off the debt, Mary Sherman did not have enough money to raise her children. "All the neighbors knew that mother could not maintain so large a family without help," Cump later wrote.

Most of the children were sent to live with different friends and relatives. Cump didn't go far. His

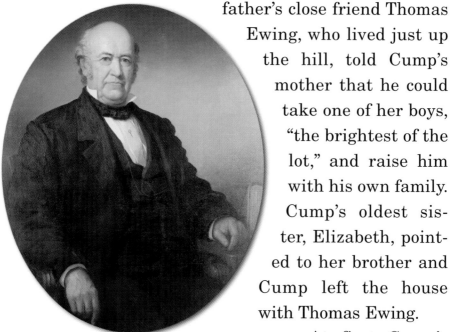

William Browne did this 1879 portrait of Thomas Ewing, whose political career flourished during the years that Cump lived with the Ewings. Sherman later referred to him as an "intellectual giant."

father's close friend Thomas Ewing, who lived just up the hill, told Cump's mother that he could take one of her boys, "the brightest of the lot," and raise him with his own family. Cump's oldest sister, Elizabeth, pointed to her brother and Cump left the house with Thomas Ewing.

At first Cump's life didn't change all that much. He still saw his brothers and sisters every day. He and the oldest Ewing boy, Philemon, ate frequently at his mother's house. Gradually, though, his brothers and sisters left the Sherman home. His oldest brother, Charles, went to live with an uncle and studied law. Elizabeth got married. Lampson, who was eight, went to live with a friend of their father's in Cincinnati. John, who was six, stayed with their mother two more years and then went to live with a cousin of their father's who lived 50 miles (80 km) away. Only the three youngest children stayed home.

At the Ewings' home, Cump had a new set of brothers and sisters: Phil, Ellen, Hugh, and later the newborn Tom. Thomas Ewing's wife, Maria, was a devout Catholic. When Cump came to live with them, she wanted him baptized as a Catholic. Cump's mother gave her permission, so the next time a priest was in town, Cump was baptized. The priest asked the boy's name. "Tecumseh," he was told.

The priest said the name had to be either the name of a saint or a name from the Bible. Since it was St. William's Day, the priest picked the name William. After that, Cump signed his name "William T. Sherman" or "W. T. Sherman." His family and friends, however, still called him Cump.

Although Cump was baptized and took part when Maria Ewing instructed her children in the Catholic faith, his own family was Episcopalian and he never seemed to have considered himself a Catholic. Cump was not the only non-Catholic in the household. Thomas Ewing was not a Catholic either. "To him it made little difference whether the religion was Methodist, Presbyterian, Baptist or Catholic," Cump later said.

The Ewings were a well-off family who became wealthier over the years. In 1831, Thomas Ewing was elected to the U.S. Senate. He moved to Washington for part of the year, but his family stayed in Ohio. Even from afar, Ewing closely supervised his children's education. He placed particular emphasis on the importance of reading and encouraged the children to read novels and plays as well as serious works. Because of this influence, Cump was an avid reader his entire life.

When Cump was fifteen, his twelve-year-old brother, John, had begun to feel uncomfortable at their father's cousin's house. The cousin now had children of his own to provide for, so John moved back to their mother's home. Once John was home, he attached himself to Cump, who often let him tag along.

The brothers seemed to be very different. Cump was quiet and obedient. John was wild and hot tempered. Many years later, John recalled of his older brother, "At that time, he was a steady student, quiet in his manners and easily moved by sympathy or affection. I was regarded as a wild, reckless lad, eager in controversy and ready to fight. No one could then anticipate that he was to be a great warrior and I a plodding lawyer and politician."

As a senator, Thomas Ewing was able to get Cump a free college education. Each year, Ewing could appoint a deserving young man from Ohio to the U.S. Military Academy at West Point, the military college that trained officers for the U.S. Army. Even though a West Point education was free, there was little competition among young Ohioans for West Point appointments. Most Ohioans were suspicious of the military and wanted nothing to do with it. Despite most young Ohioans' lack of interest, West Point was difficult to get

George Catlin published this engraving of the U.S. Military Academy at West Point in 1828. When Cump arrived at West Point and saw the older cadets marching on the parade ground, he wrote to Hugh Ewing that the cadets were "stepping as one man—all forming a line." New cadets were issued a math book, a bucket, a lamp, a broom, and two blankets.

into and offered its students one of the best educations then available in America.

Cump entered West Point in the summer of 1836, when he was sixteen. He found his studies easy, but he never mastered all the strict rules and regulations. Every year, he piled up a large number of demerits. He missed roll calls, failed to keep his uniform clean and his room neat, saluted improperly, visited other cadets' rooms when he was supposed to be in his own, left campus without permission, and cooked food in his room.

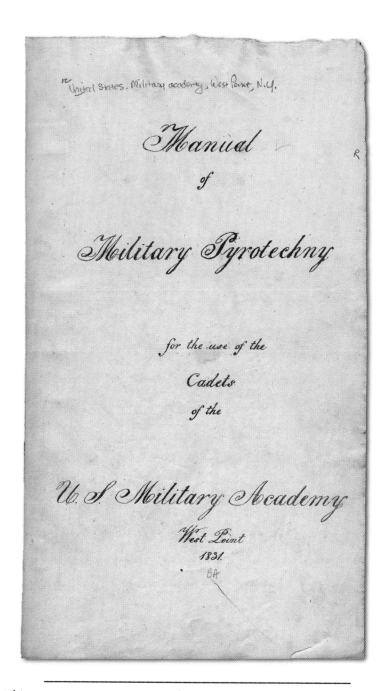

This 1831 West Point manual on military pyrotechny instructed
cadets on the preparation of ammunition and fuses to be used in
weapons such as cannons and rockets.

"I remember him as a bright-eyed red-headed fellow who was always prepared for a lark of any kind and who usually had a grease-spot on his pants," William S. Rosecrans, the future Union general, said years later.

West Point food was terrible. Cadets supplemented it by sneaking boiled potatoes out of the mess hall, and cooking them into a hash over the fires in their rooms. "He was considered the best hash-maker at West Point, and this, in our day, was a great honor," Rosecrans remembered of Cump Sherman.

Cadets often gathered in Cump's room for food and talk. Cump, who had been quiet as a boy, was extremely talkative as an adult, and at West Point "Old Cump" was considered one of the school's best storytellers.

While he was at West Point, he received many letters from Ellen, the Ewings' oldest daughter, and from his brother John. John left school when he was fourteen to work as a surveyor, a person who makes maps and takes measurements of the land. Later he studied law with his oldest brother, Charles, and their uncle Jacob Parker. Both Charles and Jacob were good lawyers, but neither liked to appear in court, so John started appearing for them while he was still a teenager.

In those days, West Point cadets received more of an engineering education than a military one. Only in Cump's final year at West Point did he take courses in artillery and infantry tactics.

Cump's grades were always near the top of his class. He was particularly good at drawing, French, and engineering. In July 1840, he graduated sixth in his class. He would have been fourth had it not been for his demerits.

Thomas Ewing urged him to leave the army and prepare for a civilian job. Cump, however, liked the camaraderie, or the spirit of friendship, that he found in the army and insisted on staying. He returned to Lancaster for the summer before going to Fort Pierce in Florida, where he had been assigned as a second lieutenant.

3. Missing the Mexican War

In Florida, where William T. Sherman was assigned to military duty, the second Seminole War had been going on since 1835. Escaped slaves from Florida and Georgia often headed for Seminole Territory, where they were welcomed as members of the Seminole Indian Nation.

Local slave owners had been calling for the federal government to put an end to this, and the result had been the Seminole War. By the time Sherman arrived, however, the war was winding down. Many of the Seminoles had been forcibly moved west to Oklahoma, and the army was cutting off the food supply of those who were still resisting. Years later, during the Civil War, Sherman would remember what an effective weapon cutting off the enemy's food supplies could be.

Sherman was promoted to first lieutenant in 1841. After a few brief assignments, he was transferred to Fort Moultrie in Charleston, South Carolina, in 1842. Sherman loved South Carolina. "Our life there was of strict garrison duty, with plenty of leisure for hunting and

This 1861 watercolor, *Fort Moultrie, Charleston Harbor,* was created by A. Vizitelly. The artist has drawn a view of the fort from inside the fort walls, with Charleston Harbor visible in the background. The stone and brick walls of the fort were 12 feet (3.5 m) high, and the parapet along the top could hold fifty cannons.

social entertainment," he later recalled. He spent a lot of time painting and exploring the area. Military officers were popular in Charleston, so Sherman was also drawn into Southern society where he made many good friends.

In 1843, he received a three-month leave of absence. He visited Lancaster, Ohio, and it was then that his relationship with Ellen Ewing changed. Although they had written to each other regularly since he had gone to West Point, their letters had not been romantic. During this visit, however, they became engaged.

At first Maria Ewing objected because the two had grown up together. Then she decided that, because Sherman and Ellen weren't really related, it was all right. Ellen was extremely bright and could be stubborn. She was one of the few people who could keep up with Sherman in a discussion. She was also a devout Catholic and hoped to convert Sherman. Their religious differences would be a problem throughout their lives.

Ellen was the daughter of a wealthy man and was not prepared for living on the limited salary of a soldier. Ellen and her parents urged Sherman to leave the

This colored engraving, *City of Charleston, South Carolina, Looking Across Cooper's River,* was created by George Cooke and William James Bennett in 1838. Many of the ships that came into Charleston Harbor transported the city's chief exports, cotton and rice.

This portrait of Ellen Ewing Sherman, created eighteen years after she married Sherman, was painted by George Peter Alexander Healy in 1868. Sherman wrote a letter to Thomas Ewing in 1844 and formally requested permission to marry Ewing's daughter.

Army and find a job with better pay. Sherman refused, and Ellen accepted his decision.

Sherman returned to the Army an engaged man. He was posted to Georgia to investigate the claims of 1,500 Georgia militiamen, who wanted the Army to pay for horses they said were killed in the Seminole War. The army suspected that many of these horses had returned to Georgia in perfect health. While tracking the horses down, Sherman became very familiar with the Georgia countryside. This familiarity would become valuable to him during the Civil War.

Sherman returned to Fort Moultrie in 1844, and, as did most other Americans, he closely observed that year's presidential campaign. Henry Clay was the Whig candidate, and James K. Polk was the Democratic candidate. The focus of the campaign was on westward expansion, but the issue of slavery also played a big role. The Republic of Texas wanted to enter the Union. Northern Whigs were afraid that Texas would be divided into several slave states and would upset the balance of power in the Senate. Democrats favored the annexation of Texas.

To avoid alienating Northerners, Polk made it clear that he favored expansion in the North as well as in the South. A dispute with Britain over the Oregon boundary became a major Polk campaign issue. Polk promised that he would make Britain, which then controlled Canada, accept a boundary far north of where the

Canadian border is today. Whigs saw the Oregon issue as a smoke screen created to push through the annexation of Texas.

As did most military officers, Sherman strongly distrusted politicians, so he was unhappy to hear that his brother John had made a speech at a Whig rally. "What the Devil are you doing?" he wrote John. "Stump speaking! I really thought you were too decent for that."

Polk defeated Henry Clay in an extremely close election, and, in 1845, Texas was admitted as a state. In 1846, Polk sent U.S. troops into territory that had been claimed by both Texas and Mexico. A skirmish between U.S. and Mexican troops led the United States to declare war on May 11, 1846. Not everyone favored the Mexican War, though. The Texas-Mexico border had never been agreed upon, and many Northern Whigs thought that Polk had deliberately started the war by occupying disputed territory.

For Sherman, however, the war was an opportunity to advance his military career. Therefore, he was frustrated when he was sent to Pittsburgh to help recruit soldiers instead of being sent to Mexico. When he was finally transferred, Sherman was sent to California, which was then part of Mexico, but was far from the major battlegrounds.

Sherman set sail for California on July 14, 1846. Sherman's ship did not reach California until January 26, 1847. By then the United States had already seized

Painting was one of Sherman's favorite hobbies, and he ranked first in his West Point drawing class. Sherman created this sketch on his 198-day voyage to California from New York in 1847. Pictured is the harbor at Rio de Janeiro, Brazil.

California. While Sherman's classmates from West Point were gaining combat experience, Sherman was taking care of paperwork and supplies.

The discovery of gold in California in the spring of 1848 made matters worse. "Gold in immense quantities has been discovered. All the towns and farms are abandoned," he wrote to his brother John. People quit their jobs to pan for gold. Supplies grew short as the farmers and service people who had previously provided them became occupied with prospecting for gold. Prices for food and shelter rose tremendously, and it became impossible for the army officers to live on their salaries.

The discovery of gold in California brought thousands
of prospectors to the state. Men who were doctors, farmers,
cooks, soldiers, and sailors deserted their professions, and often
their families, for a chance to become rich in the goldfields.
Approximately 80,000 men came to California in 1849,
earning themselves the nickname the forty-niners.

"I have never been so hard up in my life," Sherman wrote to John.

In the fall of 1848, with two other officers, Sherman set up a general store near the mines, which operated until the spring of 1849. The store earned him $1,500. He later said that without this extra money, "I could not have lived through the winter."

In late 1848, Sherman and Colonel Richard B. Mason, who had become the military governor of California and had named Sherman his adjutant, or aide, sent an official letter to Washington reporting the discovery of gold. President Polk announced the discovery in a special message in December 1848, and in 1849, the California gold rush began.

With the California gold rush in full swing, Sherman got a two-month furlough in the late spring of 1849. He added to his army salary by taking various surveying jobs, which earned him $6,000.

On January 2, 1850, after three years in California, Sherman was sent east to New York. From there he joined the Ewings in Washington, where preparations were being made for his marriage to Ellen. He and Ellen had now been engaged for seven years. Sherman was thirty, and she was twenty-six.

In the days before and after the wedding, Sherman attended the congressional debates over the Compromise of 1850. Senator Henry Clay had proposed a compromise to settle several bitterly disputed issues

This daguerreotype of Senator Henry Clay was taken by Mathew Brady around 1850. The passage of Clay's 1850 compromise might have delayed the start of the Civil War by ten years.

between the North and the South and to ward off talk of states seceding, or withdrawing, from the Union.

To satisfy the North, Senator Clay proposed that the territory of California be allowed to enter the Union as a free state and that slave trading be prohibited in Washington, D.C. To satisfy the South, he proposed that slavery be put to a popular vote in the rest of the territory acquired in the Mexican War. In addition, a fugitive slave law would be passed that would allow slave owners to capture escaped slaves who were living in free states and take them back into slavery.

Sherman asked Senator Thomas Corwin of Ohio, who had been a close friend of his father's, to take him onto the floor of Congress so that he could hear Senator Daniel Webster's speech in support of the compromise. "There can be no such thing as peaceable secession,"

Webster said in that speech. Sherman was most impressed, however, by Henry Clay, who declared that were his beloved state of Kentucky to secede from the Union, "I would shoulder my old musket and be among the first to put her down, down, down."

On May 1, 1850, Sherman and Ellen were finally married. Because Sherman was not a Catholic, they could not be married in a Catholic church. As Ellen wouldn't consider being married in any other church, they were married in the Ewings' Washington, D.C., home, with two priests officiating.

4. Leaving the Army

After spending part of the summer with his new wife, William Tecumseh Sherman became a captain in the St. Louis, Missouri, commissary department, which supplied food to soldiers in the area. In January 1851, he and Ellen had their first baby, a daughter they named Maria but always called Minnie. Although he found his work in St. Louis dull, Sherman loved the city and invested $4,000 in land there.

After a year in St. Louis, Sherman was sent to New Orleans, Louisiana, to clean up corruption in its commissary. Businessmen were bribing officers to get army contracts. Sherman put an end to the bribery by not allowing officers to sign contracts and by purchasing the army's supplies in the markets. Ellen had returned to her parents' house in Ohio to await the birth of her second child, a daughter who would be named Mary Elizabeth and nicknamed Lizzie. By the time Ellen joined him in New Orleans, Sherman was bored with his job and was worried that he was not earning enough to support his wife and children.

A friend from California, Henry S. Turner, had become a banker in St. Louis. Turner and his business partner, James H. Lucas, asked Sherman to be the business manager of a bank they were opening in San Francisco. Sherman took a six-month leave of absence from the army to check out the California job.

Sherman was not impressed with how the bank was organized. After Turner and Lucas agreed to provide more money to get the bank running properly and offered Sherman a salary of $5,000 per year and one-eighth of the profits, Sherman resigned from the army and accepted the position. Sherman and Ellen

Sherman named his daughter Mary Elizabeth "Lizzie" Sherman, for his mother and sister. This photograph was taken when Lizzie was nine years old.

moved to San Francisco in the fall of 1853. They took Lizzie with them, but Minnie stayed in Ohio with Ellen's parents.

Sherman prospered at the bank, but Ellen hated San Francisco. Streets were unpaved and prices were shockingly high. "Cump gives me $75 every Monday . . . and yet by Saturday night there is seldom any left— and I am not extravagant," she wrote to her parents.

Sherman had always been prone to asthma, and it seemed to be worse in the damp, cold air of San Francisco. Ellen was sure his health would improve if they lived somewhere else. Even the birth of another baby in June 1854, a boy named William and nick-named Willy, did not make Ellen any happier.

Many San Francisco businesses, including banks, had trouble during the winter of 1854–1855. Lucas, Turner & Company was better prepared than were the other banks.

In February 1855, several banks were rumored to be near failure, and a run on all of San Francisco's banks began. At that time, bank deposits were not insured by the government. If there were any rumors that a bank was in trouble, people would rush in and remove their money, starting a run on the bank. By asking friends to make payments on their bank loans and by urging key depositors to leave their money in the

Sherman drew this 1855 sketch of his newly built San Francisco home on the back of a Lucas, Turner & Company bank check.

bank, Sherman was able to keep the Lucas and Turner bank open.

In April 1855, Ellen insisted on visiting her parents and Minnie in Ohio. Lizzie and Willy remained with their father in California. When Ellen returned in late November, Sherman's asthma was so bad that she was afraid he would not survive the winter. The bank was not making money, and business worries were bothering him so much that he was barely sleeping.

Another son, Thomas, was born in October 1856. In early 1857, Lucas and Turner decided to close the bank. They then put Sherman in charge of a bank they were opening in New York.

Sherman and Ellen returned east. Ellen and the children stayed with her parents in Ohio while Sherman worked on getting the bank set up in New York. In August 1857, however, a business crisis hit New York. That October, Lucas and Turner closed their New York operation. Sherman was out of a job.

While Sherman was in San Francisco, his brother John had been elected to the House of Representatives in 1854 as a congressman from Ohio. He had won the election by denouncing the Kansas-Nebraska Act, which had been passed in 1854. This act allowed the residents of Kansas and Nebraska to vote on whether they wished to allow slavery within their borders, even though, under the terms of the 1820 Missouri Compromise, both should have been free states.

Proslavery and antislavery activists had poured into Kansas, and, by 1856, the two sides were practically at war.

Sherman was thinking of moving to Leavenworth, Kansas, where Tom Ewing Jr., Ellen's brother, was managing Thomas Ewing's Kansas property and setting up a law office of his own. Tom was also becoming involved in antislavery politics. Because Tom's political activities were taking so much time, he needed help running his office. Sherman moved to Leavenworth, took over managing the properties, and studied law on his own. Ellen didn't like Kansas any more than she had liked San Francisco, as living conditions were rough. She and the children stayed with Sherman in Kansas for five months and then returned to Ohio.

Sherman looked for another job. The first possibility that came through was from a new college, the Louisiana Seminary of Learning and Military Academy, which later became Louisiana State University. The academy needed a superintendent. Sherman moved to Louisiana in the fall of 1859, while Ellen and the children stayed in Ohio.

Sherman was popular with most of the students, and his talent for organization made him perfect for getting a college up and running.

However much he enjoyed this position, Sherman was beginning to see that the job could not last. Ellen, he knew, would be unhappy in Louisiana. The academy

This is an image of the Louisiana Seminary of Learning and Military Academy. In a letter to his daughter, Sherman described the seminary building as a "great Big Castle like those in which the Knights used to live." Sherman supervised the building of the academy, and by the first year the school had sixty-two cadets.

was in a remote area, far from stores or a Catholic church. The political situation also was becoming difficult. John Sherman's name was in the newspapers frequently, and he was taking a forceful position against slavery.

Sherman's politics were very different from his brother's, but they were also very different from those of his Southern friends. Louisianans were talking openly about secession, and Sherman considered the breakup of the Union unthinkable.

The Louisiana Seminary of Learning and Military Academy is
shown in the window in the upper right corner of this painting.
The board of the Academy commissioned this 1860 painting
of Sherman to honor his role in founding the school.

As the 1860 presidential campaign got under way, it became obvious that a crisis was approaching. In Ohio, John campaigned for Abraham Lincoln, who opposed allowing slavery to spread into any more states. Ellen wrote from Ohio that she, too, was becoming a Lincoln supporter. "Aren't you afraid they'll hang me for an abolitionist when I go south?" she wrote.

After Lincoln won the election, Sherman anxiously watched as Louisiana drifted closer to secession. On Christmas Eve, 1860, news that South Carolina had seceded reached the academy. David Boyd, a teacher at the college, later recalled Sherman's response. "You don't know what you are doing," Sherman declared. "You are rushing into war with one of the most powerful, ingeniously mechanical and determined people on earth—right at your doors. You are bound to fail."

The secessions of Mississippi, Florida, Alabama, and Georgia followed. Sherman remained at the academy. Then Sherman learned that the governor of Louisiana was sending arms that the state had seized from the federal arsenal at Baton Rouge, Louisiana, to the seminary. Sherman resigned. "On no earthly account will I do any act or think any thought hostile or in defiance to the old government of the United States," he wrote to the governor. Sherman left Louisiana in February and was back in Ohio by March.

In the North, though, Sherman felt displaced. While Southerners had been rushing toward war, Northerners seemed to have ignored the crisis. John, who had recently been elected to the Senate by the state of Ohio, asked Sherman to come to Washington, D.C. John planned to introduce his brother to important people and help him to find another job. One of the people that John introduced Sherman to was Abraham Lincoln.

Sherman was not impressed. He was so angry about the offhand way that Lincoln seemed to be dealing with the crisis that he remembered little about the meeting. It was John who later recalled that Sherman offered his services to the army and was turned down. Lincoln said that he hoped to solve the matter without soldiers.

Sherman left Washington. He was forty-one years old. He had worked as a soldier, a banker, a real-estate manager, a lawyer, and a college president. Not one single job had lasted. His children and his wife were spending more time in her parents' house than they were with him. Sherman felt like a failure.

5. A Disastrous Year

John did find a job for his brother. William T. Sherman was offered the chief clerkship in the War Department. This position could have been a stepping-stone back into the army, but Sherman turned it down. Instead, he took a job in St. Louis running a streetcar company.

On April 12, 1861, the Civil War began. Confederate forces attacked Fort Sumter in South Carolina. Anger swept the North, and Lincoln asked for three-month volunteers to serve in the army. Sherman was disgusted, as three-month volunteers would return home before they were properly trained.

John urged him to go to Ohio, raise a regiment, and become its colonel. John would then be able to get him appointed as commander of all Ohio's troops. Sherman turned him down. The governor of Ohio named George McClellan instead, and within three months McClellan was general in chief of the U.S. Army.

John went to Ohio and raised a regiment himself. Sherman's oldest brother, Charles, raised several regiments. Sherman continued with his new job in St. Louis.

Even those who knew him well were unsure why Sherman turned down the military jobs. Perhaps he was sulking because his first offer to serve had not been accepted. Perhaps he was waiting for evidence that the North was taking the war seriously.

Meanwhile, the U.S. Army was disorganized. As the Southern states seceded, Southern army officers began to resign. Northerners were shocked to learn how thoroughly Southerners had dominated the army. The three generals that Winfield Scott, the commanding general of the U.S. Army, considered the most talented, Robert E. Lee, Joseph Johnston, and Albert Sidney Johnston, had all resigned to serve the Confederacy. Winfield Scott was a smart military man, but his age and health made it impossible for him to lead the Union troops. Unfortunately, there was no other clear choice.

By May, Sherman had finally decided to return to the army. He was named colonel of the Thirteenth Regular Infantry, based near Washington, D.C. As did most West Point officers, Sherman had trouble with the volunteers. The volunteers knew nothing about military matters, and they didn't like officers. Many volunteers came from cities and had never even held a gun.

In July, approximately twenty-five thousand Union troops, including Sherman's men, marched against Confederate forces at Manassas Junction, Virginia. The troops didn't know how to march. Tired soldiers stopped to rest as their officers screamed at them to keep moving. Others wandered off to pick blackberries, and their officers could not stop them.

The Confederate troops were equally unprepared. When officers tried to get them to dig trenches, they refused. Gentlemen didn't dig.

On July 21, 1861, the Battle of Bull Run began. At 3:00 P.M., the Union seemed to have scored an impressive victory. Then Confederate reinforcements arrived and Confederate officers were able to rally their troops and repulse the Union attack.

Disorder marked Bull Run. Union officers were not able to organize their men to execute their battle plan.

Alfred R. Waud created this eyewitness drawing of Colonel Burnside's Union brigade attacking the Confederate batteries at Bull Run on July 21, 1861. As cameras could not yet capture moving images, newspapers and magazines relied on sketch artists for battle depictions.

The battle ended when Union volunteers decided they had had enough and left the field in a decided retreat. Sherman's men were among the last to leave. When the Confederate cavalry tried to follow, his men fired and did enough damage to keep the Confederates from following.

The Union retreat soon turned into chaos. Troops heading back toward Washington got mixed in with panicking Washingtonians who had traveled to Virginia to see the battle but were now fleeing. "I have read of retreat before, have seen the noise and confusion of crowds of men at fires and shipwrecks, but nothing like this," Sherman wrote. "It was as disgraceful as words can portray."

Sherman was humiliated. He felt that every Union officer who had taken part in the battle deserved to be fired. Even though he was praised for performing better than most of the other officers and was promoted to brigadier general, Sherman felt that he had failed. "For us to say we commanded that army is no such thing," he wrote. "They did as they pleased."

Not long after Bull Run, General Robert Anderson, who had been the hero of Fort Sumter and had been put in charge of the Union effort in Kentucky, asked that Sherman be made his second in command.

Sherman, who hadn't gotten along with the volunteers in the Thirteenth Regular Infantry, was happy to leave Washington. The situation in Kentucky, however, was very tense. Kentucky had not seceded from the Union, but it was a slave state, and many of its residents sympathized with the Confederates. If the Confederates took Kentucky, their northern defensive line would be the Ohio River. It would be extremely difficult for the Union to attack them, because the Union troops would have to cross the river.

It was crucial that the Union hold the state, but there were not enough troops to defend it. Not long after Sherman arrived, Anderson became ill from the stress of being responsible for defending Kentucky. He resigned. That left Sherman as the commanding officer.

At that point, there was no overall plan for winning the war. General Winfield Scott had come up with a plan that emphasized a thrust down the Mississippi River. It had been rejected, however, and Scott had been eased into retirement when General George McClellan had trouble working under him.

McClellan was focused on taking Richmond, Virginia, the capital of the Confederacy. The Lincoln administration wanted Kentucky held at all costs and hoped for a push into eastern Tennessee.

Sherman's troops in Kentucky were no better prepared than the troops at Bull Run had been. Remembering that disaster, Sherman pressed the men hard. He worked himself to the point of exhaustion, slept less than three hours a night, smoked too many cigars, and barely ate.

1: BACON'S MILITARY MAP OF AMERICA. 1:

BACON'S
MILITARY MAP OF THE
UNITED STATES
Showing the
FORTS & FORTIFICATIONS

There were constant rumors that Confederate forces were about to attack and there were wild estimates about the number of Confederate troops in Kentucky. Sherman believed them all. He worried about sending unprepared men to their deaths. He feared that he would be personally responsible for the breakup of the Union if he didn't properly defend Kentucky. Sherman fired off a stream of letters to everyone he could think of in Washington, warning them of the approaching disaster.

Simon Cameron, secretary of war, was photographed in the 1860s. When Sherman requested more men, Cameron replied, "Great God! Where are they to come from?"

Secretary of War Simon Cameron went to Kentucky to assess the situation. Sherman showed him a map of the United States. In the East, McClellan had 100,000 men. In the West, there were 60,000 men. Sherman had only 18,000 men in the central area and was covering far more territory. To defend the area, he needed 60,000 men. To go on the offense, he needed 200,000 men. Cameron called it an insane request and spread the word in Washington that

Opposite: Bacon's military map of the United States was published in London in 1862. Free, or nonslaveholding, states are colored in green, slaveholding states that did not secede are colored in yellow, and slaveholding states that seceded are colored in pink.

Sherman was acting irrationally. Sherman knew he should be doing something, but he was afraid that a move on his part could lead to a serious defeat. "To advance would be madness and to Stand still folly," he wrote to Ellen. "The idea of going down to History with a fame such as threatens me nearly makes me crazy, indeed, I may be so now."

In November 1861, knowing that he was near his breaking point, Sherman asked to be relieved of his command. The request was granted, but as he waited for General Don Carlos Buell to replace him, his condition seemed to worsen. His aide telegraphed Ellen.

Ellen left for Louisville, Kentucky, immediately. When she arrived, she found Sherman in the middle of an emotional crisis. She wrote to John, "He thinks the whole country is gone irrevocably & ruin & desolation are at hand — For God's sake do what you can to cheer him." John also rushed to Louisville, and they both stayed until Buell arrived. Both Sherman's wife and his brother were still anxious when he was sent to St. Louis to serve under General Henry W. Halleck.

Halleck, who had known Sherman at West Point and in California, became concerned as well after Sherman reported to him. When Ellen didn't hear from Sherman for ten days, she went to St. Louis. Halleck met with Ellen and suggested that Sherman take a furlough. "Take your husband home, and don't let him talk politics or read newspapers for two weeks," Halleck told her.

Sherman returned to Ohio with Ellen. A week later, several newspapers reported that he had been removed from his command because he was insane. The *Cincinnati Commercial* article appeared under the headline "General William T. Sherman Insane."

Sherman was extremely depressed and felt that he had disgraced his entire family. Nevertheless, away from the pressure of being in charge at Kentucky, Sherman began to recover.

This portrait of Major General Henry W. Halleck was taken by John A. Scholten in the 1860s.

If he had not had several powerful relatives, including John Sherman, Charles Sherman, Thomas Ewing, and Tom Ewing Jr., his military career would probably have ended. As soon as his relatives knew he would recover, they swung into action. They pressured the *Cincinnati Commercial* to print a retraction, or a statement saying that the newspaper had been wrong. His relatives wrote and spoke to everyone they knew in his defense.

On December 17, Sherman returned to duty. During his furlough, Sherman had had time to think about what had happened. He realized that he had exaggerated the Confederates' strength in Kentucky, and he was determined that he would never make that mistake again.

6. Grant Shows the Way

William T. Sherman reported back to General Halleck and was assigned to train volunteers. This time, the volunteers liked him. Rumors that Sherman was crazy were still being discussed, but the volunteers appreciated a general who didn't care what their uniforms looked like and concentrated on what really mattered: teaching his soldiers how to march and fight as a unit.

Halleck was convinced that controlling the Tennessee River, which flowed through the center of Tennessee, would open the way to the Mississippi River and was the key to success in the West. Halleck authorized fifteen thousand men, led by General Ulysses S. Grant, to take control of Fort Henry on the Tennessee River and Fort Donelson on the nearby Cumberland River.

Grant quickly took Fort Henry. Then on February 13, 1862, he laid siege to the more powerful Fort Donelson. Keeping Grant supplied with troops and food was crucial, and Halleck assigned Sherman to the job. Sherman successfully forwarded troops and food to

General Grant, and this marked the beginning of a friendship between the two men.

On February 16, Fort Donelson fell. The North was now in control of the Tennessee River. The victory at Fort Donelson took the pressure off Kentucky. The Confederates were also forced to abandon much of Tennessee as well. General Halleck was put in charge of all the western armies.

The next Union objective was to take Corinth, Mississippi, just over the Tennessee border. The first step toward this goal was to control the Memphis and Charleston Railroad. Railroads were extremely important during the Civil War because they were used to supply and move troops. Cutting

Grant's victory at Fort Donelson was the first decisive Union victory of the Civil War. Military textbooks had advised that forts should not be attacked without at least a five-to-one advantage in men. Grant attacked Fort Donelson with about the same number of men as were inside the fort and proved that the textbooks were wrong. When the Confederate general Simon B. Buckner asked for terms, Grant thrilled the North with his reply: "No terms but unconditional and immediate surrender can be accepted." Buckner surrendered, and Grant captured between twelve thousand and fifteen thousand prisoners. The North had a new hero, "Unconditional Surrender" Grant.

off the enemy's railroad line could trap the enemy in a dangerous position.

Sherman took command of the advance guard, the first soldiers to enter an area. He and his men traveled by steamboat on the Tennessee River from Savannah, Tennessee, to Pittsburg Landing in southern Tennessee, where they disembarked. Because rains and flooding made it impossible to reach the railroad, Sherman was ordered to return to Pittsburg Landing. He was told to wait for other troops to arrive before marching on Corinth. Sherman settled his men 2.5 miles (4 km) from the landing, near Shiloh Church.

Battle of Shiloh was created by Thure de Thulstrup in 1888. Casualties in this battle were enormous: 13,000 Union soldiers and 11,000 Confederate soldiers. As antiseptics were not yet a medical standard, unsanitary conditions caused many more deaths among the wounded.

Confederates were gathering in the area as well. Sherman guessed that the Confederates had twenty thousand men. There were actually forty thousand men, and their commander, Albert Sidney Johnston, was planning a daring attack.

The Confederates planned to launch a surprise attack, push back the unprepared Union forces, camped between the Tennessee River and a creek, and force them into the swamp. There would be no escape.

Neither army at Shiloh had much battle experience, however. During their march, the Confederates moved so slowly and made so much noise that officers urged Johnston to call off the attack. The Union officers assumed that the noise was being made by scattered Confederate forces and not by an attacking army. Sherman, who was closest to the planned point of attack, had learned his lesson about believing rumors. He refused to take the reports of large numbers of Confederate forces in the area seriously. Grant, not aware of any particular danger, was in Savannah, Tennessee, 9 miles (14 km) away.

By Saturday, April 5, 1862, the Confederate troops had all arrived. They got up early Sunday morning and lined up to attack. Union soldiers heard shots popping as the undisciplined Confederates lined up, but they assumed the sounds came from pickets, or from the advance guards, who often fired warning shots if they thought they heard something. Sherman continued to ignore reports that Confederates might be approaching.

It was not until Sherman saw the full Confederate force marching toward them that he realized they were under attack. The nervous colonel of the Ohio Fifty-third had already sounded a drum roll to get his men to line up for battle. Sherman ordered the men of the Fifty-third to hold their line at all costs and began rushing in reinforcements.

As the battle began, Sherman put together a line of men. It fell back slowly, and the other Union generals who were camped near the river began moving in with their own forces. The Confederates were not able to crush the line, but, as the day progressed, the Union forces were gradually pushed back. Because no one had dug trenches that would give the troops some protection from enemy bullets, the slaughter was horrible.

Sherman was both brilliant and calm once the battle began. Shots whizzed around him as he reorganized regiments and plugged up holes in his line. He seemed so sure of himself that his men gradually gained confidence. When Grant, who had set off from Savannah as soon as he heard gunshots, visited Sherman at around 10:00 A.M. he saw no reason to remain. Sherman had the situation under control.

Sherman came close to being killed that day. Several horses were shot from under him and a bullet hit his

This horse, which was probably a cavalry horse killed
in battle, was sketched in pencil by the Civil War
combat artist Alfred Waud during the 1860s.

hand, but nothing affected his concentration. Many
regiments broke ranks and ran, but others regrouped
and returned to the battle.

The Confederates were having problems as well. The
slaughter was so horrible that the Confederate troops
began to lose heart. To inspire them, General Johnston
led an attack himself. A bullet hit him in the leg. He
ignored it, and then suddenly fell off his horse and died.
When his officers cut off his boot, it was filled with
blood. He had bled to death.

The day ended with the Union line pushed back, but not into the swamp. Confederates were sleeping in Union tents, but they had lost their commanding officer.

Late that night, William Tecumseh Sherman recalled later, he went looking for Grant to urge him to move the army out of its dangerous position. When he found Grant, leaning against a tree and smoking a cigar, something made him avoid mentioning a retreat. Years later, Sherman recalled, "I opened up with, 'Well, Grant, we've had the devil's own day, haven't we?' 'Yes,' he said with a short, sharp puff of the cigar; 'lick 'em tomorrow, though.'"

Grant had noticed that when two armies fight to a standstill, the one that wins the battle is usually the one that attacks first the next day. Grant made sure that the Union army attacked first the next morning, and, as predicted, it was the Confederates who retreated. The Union had won the battle.

At first the news brought joy to the North. Joy was replaced by dismay, however, when people learned how costly the victory had been. Never before had there been so many American deaths in a single battle.

Newspapers blamed Grant. They reported that Grant had arrived late to the battle because he was drunk, and that Union forces were so unprepared that soldiers were slaughtered in their tents. Though most of what the newspapers wrote was not true, Grant was removed from his command.

On May 1, Sherman was promoted to major general because he had performed so well during the Battle of Shiloh. When Sherman learned that Grant was packing to go home, he went to talk to him.

Grant told him, "I have stood it as long as I can and can endure it no longer." Sherman told Grant that a year earlier, when newspapers had called him insane, he had almost quit. If Grant stayed, he would probably get another chance to command. If he left, his military career would be finished. Grant decided to stay.

Corinth was taken without a battle. The Union then controlled all of Tennessee. In July 1862, Sherman was put in charge of Memphis, Tennessee. He ordered that schools, stores, and churches be reopened, but he forbade merchants to send money or supplies into Confederate-held areas. Although he was still antiabolitionist, Sherman adhered to the government ruling that runaway slaves in Memphis who did not want to return to their masters could work for the Union army instead.

Late in the fall, Ellen and the children visited him in Memphis. "He looks more wrinkled than most men of 60," Ellen wrote to her father. She was happy to see, however, that Sherman was healthy and at peace with himself.

7. Triumph and Tragedy

As William Tecumseh Sherman had predicted, Grant did get another chance. His assignment was to take Vicksburg, Mississippi, the last point on the Mississippi River that was held by the Confederates.

Vicksburg sat high on a bend in the river where its guns could easily hit passing ships. The city was difficult to approach by land, because the area around it was swampy, and a strong army protected it.

Grant first tried to advance on Vicksburg from the north. In late December 1862, he had Sherman make an attack on Chickasaw Bluff, which failed. Grant came up with another plan. He moved his men over to the western side of the Mississippi on transport ships, then marched them south. Admiral David Porter ran a number of Union transport boats past Vicksburg during the dark night.

Grant's troops could now be transported back across the river to a position south of Vicksburg, from which they could more easily attack. Sherman was uneasy, as Grant was cutting himself off from his supply line.

Grant next asked Sherman to take some of the men and make the Confederates believe that the main attack was coming from the north. Near the place where Sherman had previously been defeated at Chickasaw Bluff, he had his men land noisily, cross back over the river quietly, and then land noisily again.

Confederate troops rushed to the area, away from the place where Grant was making his main attack. By the time they arrived, though, Sherman had already pulled out. Grant's move toward Vicksburg was a success, and he telegraphed Sherman to join him.

Sherman caught up with Grant's troops on May 12, 1863. He noticed that the troops were not troubled by the lack of a supply wagon. They simply helped themselves to the food growing around them.

Grant had placed himself between Vicksburg and General Joseph Johnston's relief forces, which were assembling in Jackson, Mississippi. The night that Sherman arrived, he and Grant received word that General James B. McPherson had defeated two Confederate brigades to the northeast of Jackson at the town of Raymond. Grant ordered McPherson to move on to Jackson and sent Sherman after him.

After his embarrassment at Bull Run, Sherman had drilled his men on marching, and the work paid off.

Next spread: This aerial view of the Vicksburg National Military Park was published in 1925. The black lines in the map signify the siege site where Union troops dug their trenches. The red lines show the Confederate line of defense, and the white lines show modern roads within the park.

YAZOO CANAL

LAKE CENTENNIAL
(Made in 1876)

YAZOO RIVER

VICKSBURG

NATIONAL CEMETERY

FORT HILL

VAUG

SOUTH FORT

BARTONS ★

REYNOLDS ★

CUMMINGS

Black Lines indicate the Union Trenches.
Red Lines indicate the Confederate Line of Defense.
White Lines show the Park Roads.
The Stars mark General Headquarters.

⚑ Indicates State Memorial
⊓ Indicates Arch

THE VICKSBURG NATIONA

SHOWING LINES OF SIEGE AND DEFENSE OF

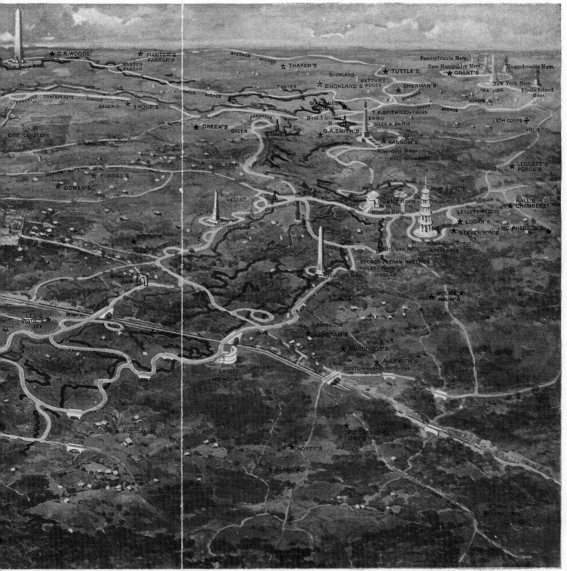

PARK AND VICINITY

NATIONAL CEMETERY IN BACKGROUND.

This portrait of the Confederate general Joseph Eggleston Johnston was painted by Benjamin Franklin Reinhart.

During the Civil War, most troops managed to move only 14 miles (22.5 km) per day under good conditions. General Sherman's troops marched 22 miles (35 km) through pouring rain in a single day. When William Tecumseh Sherman and James B. McPherson reached Jackson, Johnston's Confederate troops scattered. Sherman stayed in Jackson an extra day to destroy the railroad, the arsenal, and a cotton factory.

Grant's main force moved west. The Confederate general John C. Pemberton was defeated at the Battle of Champion's Hill on May 16. Pemberton fell back to the Big Black River.

Sherman came back from Jackson rapidly, marching 27 miles (43 km) in a single day. He reached the Big Black River in time to help Grant in a second defeat of the Confederates, who fell back to trenches just outside Vicksburg. Union attempts to storm

Vicksburg failed, but Grant's forces had surrounded the city. Because no food or supplies could reach Vicksburg, it was only a matter of time before the Confederates would have to surrender.

On June 22, Grant heard that Johnston was approaching Vicksburg with more than thirty thousand men. Sherman was sent with five divisions to meet him.

At Bear Creek, Sherman set up defenses and put on such a display of energy that he appeared to have ten times as many men. Then he sent two divisions on raids to collect or destroy all the food in the surrounding area, so that Johnston would not be able to attack without bringing along supply wagons.

Johnston did not attack. Pemberton surrendered Vicksburg on July 4, 1863. The entire Mississippi River was now in the hands of the Union.

There were rumors that Johnston was gathering a large army to take back Vicksburg. Grant gave Sherman thirty thousand men and told him to drive Johnston out of the state of Mississippi.

Sherman's march to Jackson was his first great march. The heat was almost unbearable, and Johnston's retreating soldiers had destroyed every source of water. Kerosene had been dumped into cisterns, or tanks that collected rainwater. Handles had been removed from water pumps. Farm animals had been driven into ponds and killed, and their decomposing bodies made the water undrinkable. Sherman's men survived on green

Major General Sherman was photographed by Mathew Brady's Studio in the 1860s. Sherman believed that the surrender of Vicksburg was "the first gleam of daylight in this war." Sherman told Grant, "I feel that I have labored some to secure this glorious result."

corn and rainwater. They continued to march, and on July 10, they laid siege to Jackson.

On July 16, Johnston retreated across the Pearl River. Sherman seized all of Johnston's heavy guns, destroyed the remaining war materials and the railroad, and took five hundred prisoners. Sherman's troops started back toward Vicksburg on July 20.

There was a lull in the fighting as General Halleck, who was still in charge of Union operations in the West, planned the next Union move. Sherman invited Ellen and their four oldest children to visit. Willy, who was

This Roll of Honor certificate was given to Union veterans who were part of the Army of the Cumberland. Sherman had commanded the Army of the Cumberland when he was given the responsibility of defending Kentucky. This certificate was a lithograph created by Middleton, Strobridge & Company of Cincinnati, Ohio, in 1863.

This is a portrait of Sherman's son William Ewing Sherman, who was nicknamed Willy. When Willy visited his father in Mississippi, Sherman allowed his son to ride with him during his inspection of the troops.

nine, had a particularly good time. The Thirteenth U.S. Regulars made him their honorary sergeant.

Their visit came to an end in September 1863 when a crisis developed in Chattanooga, Tennessee. The Confederate general Braxton Bragg had defeated the Union forces at Chickamauga and had driven them into Chattanooga. The Union forces were now trapped.

Sherman traveled with Ellen and the children by steamboat to Memphis. Not long after the boat set off, he noticed that something was wrong with Willy. It was typhoid fever, and the doctor on the ship didn't have the medicine to treat it. By the time they reached Memphis, Willy was failing rapidly. He died a day later.

Sherman was consumed with grief. Because of the crisis in Chattanooga, he was unable to go home with his family to attend Willy's funeral in Ohio. Sherman tried to distract himself by focusing on his work. "I must not think of him so much," he wrote to Ellen, "& yet I cannot help it."

Sherman was now in charge of the entire Army of the Tennessee. His men advanced slowly because they had been ordered to repair the Memphis & Charleston Railroad, damaged by Confederate cavalry.

Meanwhile, Confederate troops controlled the mountainside surrounding Chattanooga. Grant's plan was that Sherman would surprise Bragg with an attack on the enemy's right at Missionary Ridge while General Joseph Hooker attacked on their left at Lookout Mountain.

On November 23, 1863, Sherman's engineers quietly laid down pontoon bridges, or floating temporary bridges. The next day, his troops crossed the Tennessee River and climbed up a high ridge that faced Tunnel Hill, which lay on the northern end of Missionary Ridge. It was separated from Tunnel Hill, however, by a series of valleys. Worried that the area might be heavily fortified, Sherman paused and lost the advantage of surprise. Hooker, however, captured Lookout Mountain in what became known as the Battle Above the Clouds.

On November 25, Sherman's men finally arrived at Tunnel Hill, but the Confederates were ready for the attack and fiercely fought off any advance. Hooker moved down Lookout Mountain, crossed the Chattanooga Creek, and attacked the Confederates' left flank on Missionary Ridge, but his progress was slow.

This 1865 eyewitness drawing, *General Sherman & Staff Passing over the Pontoon Bridge,* was created by combat artist William Waud for *Harper's Weekly.* In the background are the ruins of a destroyed bridge. This wreck forced Sherman's men to create a temporary pontoon bridge to cross the Broad River.

By midafternoon, it was obvious that the battle was not going well. Grant ordered the Army of the Cumberland, which he had been holding in reserve, to advance to the rifle pits, located at the bottom of the center of Missionary Ridge. He hoped that this move would take some pressure off Sherman and Hooker.

At this point, the soldiers in the Army of the Cumberland were angry and frustrated. They had been insulted by the other units because of their loss at Chickamauga and had spent a day and a half watching the other units fight. They were furious that they weren't being allowed to take part in the battle.

When they finally got an order to attack, they charged to the rifle pits, paused briefly, then, to the shock of Grant and the officers watching with him, they kept right on going up the steep and crumbling ridge. Fifty minutes later, Union flags were flying on the ridge, and Bragg's forces were retreating in disarray. It was the most remarkable turnaround of any battle in the Civil War. Grant was hailed as a genius for an improbable victory in which luck played as important a role as skill.

8. The Atlanta Campaign

On March 9, 1864, Grant was promoted to lieutenant general, and shortly after that he was named head of all the Union armies. On March 18, Sherman was named the commanding general in the West. Grant met with Sherman and his other top Western generals in Nashville, Tennessee, to map out his plan for winning the war. All the Union armies would move in early May and go after the Confederate armies. Grant would pursue Robert E. Lee in Virginia, and Sherman would go after Joseph Johnston in Georgia.

"I will not let side issues draw me off your main plan in which I am to Knock Joe Johnston, and do as much damage to the resources of the enemy as possible," Sherman wrote to Grant. Sherman worked around the clock to organize his most ambitious mission yet. To get enough supplies for the campaign, he took over the railroad line and ran twice as many cars as the railroad men had told him was possible.

Sherman had about ninety thousand men. Johnston, who was in Dalton, Georgia, had between fifty thousand

and sixty thousand men. Because Johnston was defending his own territory and was considered a defensive genius, Sherman had a difficult task.

On May 7, the Atlanta campaign began. Sherman stationed the Army of the Cumberland and the Army of the Ohio in front of Johnston's troops. Meanwhile, General McPherson was to lead the Army of the Tennessee through a gap in the mountain range to seize the railroad at Johnston's rear. Both the Union and the Confederate armies used portions of the same railroad to bring food, ammunition, and other supplies to the troops. If the enemy seized the railroad, the opposing army would be cut off from its supplies.

To Sherman's disappointment, McPherson did not get to the railroad behind Johnston. McPherson decided that the risk to his men would be too great. Consequently, Sherman moved all of his forces around Johnston's right side. To keep Sherman's entire army from getting behind him and seizing the railroad to his rear, Johnston retreated to Resaca, which had 4 miles (6 km) of entrenchments. Sherman took over the stretch of railroad between Dalton and Resaca, and on May 13, Sherman's forces formed a semicircle around Johnston's troops. The next morning the fighting began.

The battle continued until May 15. Union forces then managed to lay a pontoon bridge over the Oostanaula River and threatened Johnston's railroad and telegraph connections. Johnston was forced to drop back again.

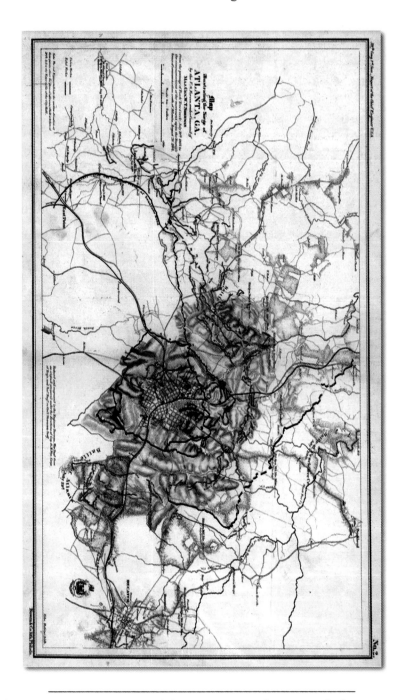

This 1866 map was created from an original map made by Captain O. M. Poe, a member of Sherman's Corps of Engineers, during the siege of Atlanta. The path of Sherman's troops toward Atlanta is marked, as are entrenchments, roads, railroads, and towns.

The pattern of the Atlanta campaign had been set. Johnston would drop back into a strong defensive position. Sherman would flank him, or move around his side, and Johnston would be forced to drop back again to keep Sherman from trapping his men.

At this point it was becoming clear just how well Sherman had prepared for the campaign. Johnston learned that there was no point in burning bridges as he retreated. Sherman carried his own. His men could lay down makeshift bridges so quickly that he barely lost any time. Broken railroad tracks were repaired instantly, and food and mail kept coming through.

Sherman studied the land before ordering an attack to avoid risking any more lives than were necessary. He seemed to know every detail of every operation, and he made certain that each soldier had what he needed to do his job properly. The soldiers nicknamed him Uncle Billy, because he seemed to look after them like an uncle.

Sherman slept only four hours a night and worked the rest of the time organizing the details of the campaign. During the day he rode beside the troops, carefully staying off the road so he didn't crowd his men. Sherman did, however, manage a few hours of catnaps by the side of the road while his troops marched.

In late May, Johnston dropped back to Allatoona Pass, an impassable mountain area. Years before, when Sherman had investigated the dead-horse claims in Georgia, he had spent a good deal of time in that area.

Sherman at Federal Fort No. 7 in Atlanta, Georgia, in the fall of 1864. This photograph was taken by George N. Barnard, the official photographer of the chief engineer's office. Most of these documentary photos were destroyed in the Atlanta fire that November.

Sherman threaded his men around the pass. His lead troops almost got behind Johnston, and Johnston was again forced to retreat.

As Johnston moved back toward Atlanta, nervous Confederate leaders demanded that he fight Sherman. Johnston realized, however, that his best hope was to retreat slowly and try to catch Sherman in a mistake.

Johnston also knew that Abraham Lincoln was having his own problems in the North. Grant had relentlessly attacked Lee and had lost sixty-five thousand men.

Northerners were not happy. If Johnston could keep Sherman from scoring a major victory before the election, Lincoln would not be reelected, and a new Northern president might be willing to negotiate a truce with the Confederacy.

Sherman had avoided frontal assaults up to this point, but at Kennesaw Mountain he noticed that Johnston's lines were thin in the center and strong on the flanks. He decided to surprise Johnston on June 27 with a frontal assault. The assault was a failure; 2,600 of Sherman's men were killed or wounded, while the Confederates lost only 522 men. Sherman called off the attack and returned to flanking.

On July 9, Johnston retreated to the Chattahoochee River. Sherman's men crossed the Chattahoochee, and Johnston pulled back farther to Peach Tree Creek.

The Confederates had had enough of Johnston's retreating. On July 17, 1864, the Confederate president, Jefferson Davis, relieved Johnston of his command and appointed General John Bell Hood in his place.

On July 20, Hood attacked the Union troops. The Union lost 1,700 men, but the Confederates lost 4,800. On July 22, just outside Atlanta, Hood attacked again, and the fighting was fierce. The Union lost 3,722 men. The Confederates lost at least 7,500. Sherman swung the Army of the Tennessee southwest of the city, and it occupied the Confederate trenches. On July 28, Hood attacked again, and the Union forces once again fought him off. The Union lost only 632 men. The Confederates may have lost as many as 3,000. Sherman's army paused just outside Atlanta, and each side waited for the other to make a move.

On August 25, Sherman began moving his entire army around the back of the city to destroy the railroad. At first it looked as if the Union army had withdrawn, and the citizens of Atlanta rejoiced. Then, as Union forces moved south, destroying the railroad as they went, Hood realized that if his men stayed in Atlanta, they would starve.

At 2:00 A.M. on September 2, the Confederates abandoned the city. Before they left, they destroyed five locomotives and eighty-one boxcars. The Union forces took over the city. "So Atlanta is ours," Sherman telegraphed, "and fairly won."

The news that Atlanta had fallen replaced gloom with glee in the North. Most people, watching Grant's Virginia campaign, had not noticed how close Sherman was to Atlanta, a vital commercial and industrial city deep in the Southern interior. Joyous Northerners realized something that had been apparent to military men since the fall of Vicksburg: The North was winning the war.

Suddenly, Lincoln was an overwhelming favorite to win the election of 1864. The Confederacy had lost its last chance for survival. Everyone knew that Lincoln would not agree to any settlement that allowed even part of the Confederacy to continue to exist.

This photograph was taken by George N. Barnard after the Atlanta fire. David P. Conyngham, a reporter for the *New York Herald* who was present at the fire, wrote, "The streets were now in one fierce sheet of flame; houses were falling on all sides."

Sherman considered his next move. If he stayed in Atlanta, he would face the same problems defending it that Johnston and Hood had faced. If he chased Hood's army, he would have a serious problem keeping his own troops supplied. Sherman had an idea. He would ignore Hood and dare the Confederates to come after him. He would cut himself off from his supplies, live off the land, and march straight through Georgia to the sea. "If we can march a well-appointed army right through his territory, it is a demonstration to the world . . . that we have a power which [Jefferson] Davis cannot resist," Sherman wrote.

Both Grant and Lincoln were reluctant to approve the campaign. They were afraid Sherman might lose his entire army. "I can make the march, and make Georgia howl," Sherman wrote to Grant. Grant and Lincoln finally agreed to Sherman's plan.

Before he left, Sherman made sure that Atlanta would be of no further use to the Confederacy. His engineers destroyed every railroad, factory, mill, and warehouse. Sherman gave orders that churches and private homes were to be spared, but the wind spread the fire to a number of private homes. Although the city was not completely destroyed, the damage was extensive.

9. Sherman's Marches

On the morning of November 16, 1864, Sherman and sixty-two thousand soldiers departed Atlanta and moved across Georgia toward a point on the coast that had not yet been decided. Sherman told Grant to look for him between Hilton Head and Savannah by Christmas. "Having alternatives I can take so eccentric a course that no general can guess at my objective," Sherman wrote to General Halleck.

Sherman's men were divided into four corps. Each corps of men marched in a column on a different road, covering up to a 60-mile-wide (96.5-km-wide) area. Each day, the corps commander selected about thirty men to forage for food. The foragers scoured the countryside collecting food, such as sweet potatoes, hogs, and turkeys, as well as destroying supplies that might help the Confederates. At the end of the day, they were to turn everything in to the commissary and then rejoin their units. They were not to enter occupied private homes, and no one was to be hurt unless they tried to harm a Union soldier. These orders were interpreted liberally, however.

James E. Taylor's 1888 engraving depicts a Union foraging party killing the pigs and sheep of a farmer in Georgia. Hay has been loaded onto a mule to feed Union horses and mules. Foragers were ordered to stock their wagons with ten days' provisions for their regiments.

The foragers had dangerous work. If soldiers in the Confederate cavalry captured them, they could be hanged or could have their throats cut. Although the foragers could be intimidating, Sherman's men harmed few civilians. Unfortunately, some corrupt groups made up of army deserters and vagabonds also foraged. These men were called bummers.

A long line of former slaves followed Sherman's troops. The able-bodied men were hired to work in his battalion of black pioneers, which helped the soldiers

About 185,000 black soldiers fought for the Union. There were 166 black regiments.

When the Union began recruiting regiments of black soldiers, Sherman initially opposed their enlistment. His reluctance came close to insubordination, but Abraham Lincoln tolerated his behavior as Sherman had given him little trouble on other matters.

Sherman argued that the black soldiers would not be as effective as white soldiers and that his men would be unwilling to serve alongside black soldiers.

Events proved that Sherman was wrong. Although there were many Union soldiers who did not want their regiments serving alongside black regiments, most of the men made the adjustment when they saw that black regiments were performing well.

Sherman did employ a battalion of black pioneers to help with digging, chopping trees, and building roads. These were skills in which Sherman's army excelled, so their contributions should not be underrated. The former slaves who followed Sherman's troops as they marched through Georgia found Sherman friendly and approachable.

with roadwork and digging. The rest were discouraged from following because of the dangers surrounding a military operation. Sherman's policy, however, was to tolerate followers if they ignored his advice.

Northerners were fascinated by Sherman's march. They scoured Confederate newspapers looking for scraps of news. The Confederate government pressured newspapers to stop writing about Sherman, so suddenly there was no news at all. Sherman had disappeared.

On December 10, Sherman reappeared outside Savannah, Georgia, and the North rejoiced. Sherman's army was completely intact. Hood had moved into Tennessee, but on December 15 and 16, General George Thomas, left behind by Sherman to defend Tennessee, defeated Hood decisively in the Battle of Nashville. Southern morale plummeted and General Robert E. Lee began having problems with men deserting. By the morning of December 21, the Confederates had abandoned Savannah, and Union troops moved in.

Grant wanted to ship Sherman's men by boat to Virginia, where they could help him finish off Lee. Sherman proposed instead that his men march through South Carolina and North Carolina to meet up with Grant. Grant reluctantly agreed when Sherman pointed out that his men could march through the Carolinas almost as quickly as they could be transported by ship.

"I think the time has come when we should attempt the boldest moves," Sherman wrote General Halleck.

"We are not only fighting hostile armies, but a hostile people, and must make old and young, rich and poor, feel the hard hand of war."

On February 1, 1865, Sherman's forces set out. By this time, nothing could stop them. They waded through shoulder-deep water in freezing temperatures, built bridges in a few short hours, and chopped down trees to make roads through impassable areas.

South Carolina did not have the vast supplies that Georgia had, so more foraging was necessary to feed the army. Because South Carolina had started the war, the Union army treated the people roughly. There were few cases in which civilians were seriously hurt, but barns and property were burned or destroyed on a regular basis.

As Sherman's men approached Columbia, South Carolina's capital, the mood turned angry when Confederates shelled a Union camp and killed several sleeping soldiers.

When the troops entered Columbia on February 17, they found casks of whiskey and started drinking. By afternoon, much of the army was drunk. Meanwhile, the cotton that retreating Confederates had set on fire was still burning in the streets.

What happened next is still in dispute. The wind might have carried the burning cotton to some of the

Next spread: Columbia the Morning After the Fire was drawn by William Waud on February 18, 1865. Waud wrote the names of several landmarks, such as the asylum and the treasury building, above the sketch.

Columbia the morning after the fire

houses and started a blaze, or drunk and angry Union soldiers might have deliberately set houses on fire. Though Sherman and his officers did their best to put it out, the fire destroyed more than one-third of the city.

Accusations that Sherman had deliberately ordered the city destroyed are made to this day. Sherman actually had intended to destroy only the buildings that contributed to the Confederate war effort. Sherman felt little sorrow over the Columbia fire, however. He considered it an accident of war, the kind that anyone foolish enough to start a war should have expected.

As Sherman's army moved into North Carolina, the mood shifted again. North Carolina had resisted

secession. Sherman's men continued to forage, but they took only what they needed and stopped burning barns.

As the soldiers marched up through the Carolinas, their attitude toward Sherman altered. They had liked and respected him for a long time. Now, however, as he rode beside the lines, prolonged cheers rose up everywhere. His men realized how much they had accomplished and how far he had taken them.

On March 20 and 21, near Goldsboro, North Carolina, Sherman once again fought General Joseph Johnston, who had been called back into service to take command of the Confederate forces in North Carolina.

As the fighting intensified, Union general Joseph A. Mower spotted a chance to trap Johnston and cut off the only point where he could escape. General Oliver O. Howard, commander of the Army of the Tennessee, sent two divisions to support Mower. Sherman called them back. Had he followed through on Mower's opening, he could have won a devastating victory. Instead he scored a modest victory, and Johnston's army remained intact. Sherman later admitted that he had probably made an error, but he didn't seem too troubled.

Some historians believe Sherman simply made a mistake. Others think that Sherman knew the war was almost over and wanted to avoid unnecessary bloodshed so close to the war's end.

On March 25, Sherman left Goldsboro to meet with Grant in City Point, Virginia, to discuss the final moves of the war. The two generals visited Lincoln, who was on a nearby boat anchored on the James River.

When Sherman had met Lincoln before the war, he had not been impressed. This time he liked Lincoln and was pleased to learn that the president wanted to offer the South a generous peace. Once the South surrendered, Southern states would be welcomed back into the Union.

Sherman returned to North Carolina, and Grant began to cut off the last of Lee's railroad supply lines. Desperate, Lee made a final attack on Grant that failed. A Union counterattack was successful. Richmond and Petersburg fell. Lee retreated toward Danville in an attempt to join Johnston's forces in

George Healy's 1868 painting *The Peacemakers* dramatizes the meeting of (*from left to right*) Major General William T. Sherman, Lieutenant General Ulysses S. Grant, President Abraham Lincoln, and Rear Admiral David D. Porter in a cabin aboard the *River Queen*.

North Carolina, but Grant's troops beat him there, forcing Lee to surrender finally at Appomattox Courthouse, in Virginia, on April 9, 1865. Grant offered generous surrender terms, ensuring that Lee's men would be able to get home in time for spring planting.

Sherman moved his troops to Raleigh, North Carolina, and prepared to make his own final move, but on April 14 he received word that Johnston was ready to surrender.

Before Sherman boarded the railcar to meet Johnston, he was handed a telegram. Sherman swore the telegrapher to secrecy and then met with Johnston.

Sherman offered Johnston the same terms that Grant had offered Lee. Johnston wanted to do more than surrender his army, however. He wanted to negotiate an end to the entire war.

William T. Sherman wrote up the points that he thought would be acceptable. Johnston was pleased to find them extremely generous. Sherman warned him that the terms needed to be approved by the government in Washington.

When Sherman got back to camp, he told his officers the news he had read in the secret telegram. Abraham Lincoln had been assassinated at Ford's Theatre in Washington, D.C. The officers told their men and then watched them closely, fearful of a rampage. Sherman's men were so stunned and heartbroken that revenge was not an issue.

When Grant saw Sherman's peace terms, he realized that they would not be acceptable. In a cabinet meeting, Secretary of War Edwin M. Stanton angrily pointed out several problems. On some points Stanton was clearly right. A line about restoring property, for example, could have been interpreted to mean that slavery could continue. On others, Stanton was simply looking to make trouble for Sherman, whom he likely viewed as a political threat.

Grant traveled to North Carolina to explain that the agreement was not acceptable. Sherman took the news well and sent word to Johnston. Johnston then accepted the terms that Grant had offered Lee. This should have been the end of the matter.

On April 24, however, an article arranged by Stanton appeared in *The New York Times*. It reported on Sherman's flawed peace agreement and Stanton's objections, and it suggested that Sherman had been bought off by the Confederates and was involved in a plot to let Jefferson Davis escape. Other newspapers picked up the story. Fear was expressed that Sherman would march his men to Washington, D.C., and take over the government.

When Sherman saw the newspapers, he was extremely angry. He met with his top officers. One of them, Carl Schurz, recalled, "He paced up and down the room like a caged lion. . . . He lashed the Secretary of War as a mean, scheming, vindictive politician. . . . He berated the people who blamed him for what he had done as a mass of fools. . . . He railed at the press, which had altogether too much freedom."

Stanton was eager to discredit Sherman because Sherman was known to disagree with the Radical Republicans on several key issues. What Stanton didn't realize was that Sherman had absolutely no interest in a political career.

Sherman had powerful relatives, however. John hadn't agreed with Sherman's peace terms either, but he began an aggressive defense of his brother. When Sherman reached Washington, he learned he was being summoned to testify in Congress. He testified that he had thought he was fulfilling government policy, that he had kept his superiors fully informed, and that he had given the agreement to his superiors for their approval before implementing it.

After Sherman testified on May 22, two great parades took place. On May 23, the Eastern troops marched. These were soldiers who had been based

To celebrate the Union's victory, a two-day parade called the Grand Review was held along Pennsylvania Avenue in Washington, D.C. Some 150,000 troops marched past the president and his cabinet.

mainly in Virginia. On May 24, the Western troops paraded down Pennsylvania Avenue. The Western troops were the men who had served under Sherman.

Sherman's troops were a huge hit. Some had recently acquired new uniforms, while others were still in rags. Many soldiers still had bare feet, but all the men moved together with a long stride. Members of the battalion of black pioneers led each brigade and carried shovels and axes. At the very end of the parade was the Bummer Brigade, which was a caravan of mules and packhorses loaded with pots and pans, along with the pets of the soldiers.

At the parade review stand, Sherman shook hands with President Andrew Johnson and General Grant. Stanton was next in line. Sherman ignored him and moved on to the other cabinet members.

On May 25, 1865, at John's urging, Sherman released a letter to the newspapers. In it he said, "I dare the War Department to publish my official letters and reports. I assert that my official reports have been purposely suppressed while all the power of the press has been malignantly turned against me."

A few days later the reports were published, and the controversy died down. Meanwhile, Sherman's men were loudly denouncing Stanton throughout Washington. On May 30, Sherman wrote a farewell address to his men, and they were quickly demobilized and sent home.

10. Commander of the Army

After the war, William T. Sherman was assigned to the military district of St. Louis, Missouri, and was put in charge of the Far West. This posting delighted Sherman, as he had lived in St. Louis before and liked the city. He was also happy to stay out of Reconstruction politics, as the North and the South reorganized and rebuilt the governments of the Southern states after the war.

In 1867, he and Ellen had their eighth and last child, a boy named Philemon Tecumseh, who was called Cump, as was his father.

In the West, Sherman's primary interest was protecting the Union Pacific Railroad, which was completed in 1869. He considered it the key to western development.

After Grant became president in 1869, Sherman replaced Grant as commanding general of the U.S. Army. He and Ellen moved to Washington, D.C.

Although Ellen was grief-stricken when her father died in 1871, she was pleased that her father had converted to Catholicism shortly before his death. She

Above is a portrait of Sherman's family. Behind the four grandchildren are (*from left to right*) Mary Elizabeth Sherman, Thomas E. Sherman, Rachel Sherman, Ellen Sherman, Eleanor Sherman Thackara, P. Tecumseh Sherman, and Maria Sherman Fitch.

redoubled her efforts to convert Sherman, but, as always, he resisted.

His religious differences with Ellen blew up into a crisis in 1878. Shortly after their son Tom graduated from Yale Law School, Tom wrote to Sherman that he didn't want to be a lawyer. Tom wanted to be a priest, and his mother approved of his decision.

Sherman was devastated. He didn't understand how Tom could lock himself away from the world. He was so upset that he couldn't help talking about it, bitterly, to

Although Sherman objected to his son Thomas Ewing Sherman becoming a priest, he agreed with his friend Samuel Bowman, who wrote that Tom had "the right of a free man to select his own lawful calling."

all his friends. Sherman didn't speak or write to his son for two years.

In 1880, Tom returned to the United States from England, where he had been studying theology. His sister Rachel met his ship. Both siblings were nervous about how their father would react when he saw Tom. When they arrived at the house, Rachel wrote, "Tom went in & with a cry my father threw his arms about him & I left them standing, clasped in each other's arms." Although Sherman had forgiven Tom, he never accepted Tom's decision. "I feel as though his life was lost," he wrote to a friend, "and am simply amazed he does not see it as I do."

Sherman retired from the army on his birthday, February 8, 1884. He and Ellen moved back to St. Louis.

In the years after the Civil War, Sherman had occasionally been asked to run for president and had always refused. In 1884, however, the pressure from the Republican Party was immense.

This is a portrait of William Tecumseh Sherman taken in the 1880s.
In his later years, Sherman frequently indulged his lifelong love of the
theater. Attending the theater, he said, added to his "health & cheer-
fulness." Among his favorite playwrights was William Shakespeare.

Friends told him he had no choice but to accept the nomination. He received several telegrams telling him that the convention was deadlocked, and he was the only candidate on whom they could agree. He telegraphed back refusals. His final telegram said: "I will not accept if nominated and will not serve if elected." The Republicans gave up and nominated James G. Blaine. Sherman is the only man in U.S. history to turn down a near-certain chance to be president.

Many politicians expected Sherman to be denounced for refusing to serve the people as their president. Instead, he was widely admired for sticking to a decision he felt was right.

After his retirement, Sherman was in great demand as a speaker at veterans' gatherings. He never prepared his remarks, but he almost always had something interesting to say. It was at a veterans' gathering in Columbus, Ohio, on August 11, 1880, that he made his most famous statement.

He talked about how the veterans knew what couldn't be told in books. Sherman said, "There is many a boy here today who looks on war as all glory, but, boys, it is all hell."

That statement, shortened to "War is hell," was picked up by newspapers and became one of the most famous statements ever made by an American.

In the years immediately following the Civil War, Sherman was fairly popular in the South, but Southern

This portrait of Union veterans of the Civil War was taken in the 1880s. Sherman is in the front row, center. Although Sherman was an active member of the politically active veterans' group the Grand Army of the Republic, he refused offers to become the organization's president.

opinion toward him began to change in 1875, when he published his *Memoirs*.

His unapologetic recounting of the March to the Sea and the Carolina campaign thrilled Northerners, but it angered Southerners. In the late 1870s, when Southern Democrats in Congress did their best to cut funding for the army, he criticized them sharply. When some Southerners described the Civil War as a noble lost cause, Sherman made it clear he thought them foolish.

At this point, many former Confederate generals were his close friends. Sherman's sharp tongue, however, had inspired hatred among most white Southerners.

When young Cump entered Yale, Sherman and Ellen moved to New York. In New York, Sherman, who had always loved the theater, was able to attend plays four times a week. Sherman quickly developed a wide circle of friends, which included the author Mark Twain. Ellen died on November 28, 1888, and was buried next to Willy in St. Louis.

In early 1891, Sherman's asthma grew worse. On his seventy-first birthday, he developed a severe bacterial infection, and pneumonia set in. Sherman's doctor was alarmed enough to tell his daughters to notify all the family. On the night of February 11, he lost consciousness, and his children asked a priest to give him extreme unction, the last rites of the Catholic Church.

On the morning of February 13, an article appeared in *The New York Times* reporting that the children had taken advantage of John Sherman's temporary absence from the house to give extreme unction to a man who was not a Catholic. John wrote an angry response. If he had been at the house he would not have tried to prevent it. His brother was "too good a Christian and too human a man to deny his children the consolation of their religion."

This statue of William Tecumseh Sherman was created from
a bust by Augustus Saint-Gaudens. Leading Sherman is Nike,
the Greek goddess of victory. The completed bronze monument
was unveiled in New York City's Central Park on May 30, 1903.

Sherman never regained consciousness, and he died on February 14, 1891. The funeral was delayed for five days so that Tom, who was in England, could attend.

Three former presidents and all the surviving generals who had served under Sherman attended. Joseph Johnston, his old Confederate rival, was an honorary pallbearer. It was a Catholic service, and Tom, now Father Tom, was one of the priests officiating.

● ● ● ●

Looking back on Sherman's life, it is interesting to see how much he had in common with Tecumseh, the man for whom he was named. Both were great warriors and were sharply intelligent. Both had a vision of what direction history should take.

If Sherman ever gave any thought to his name and what the name meant, there is no record of it. Although he separated himself from it after the priest gave him the additional name of William, he always used Tecumseh as part of his full name.

Sherman was a man of many contradictions. He was a great general, who so dreaded sending young men to their deaths that he had an emotional crisis during the first year of the Civil War.

Sherman was the first modern general to impose war deliberately on civilians, and he is still hated in many areas of the South because of it. Far fewer people died than would have, however, had he pursued war in the old-fashioned way. Instead of destroying lives, Sherman's forces focused on the destruction of property. During his marches through Georgia and the Carolinas, marches that played a crucial role in destroying the Confederacy, few people were killed.

Unfortunately, some of the most vicious practices of modern warfare may have their roots in Sherman's campaigns. In more recent conflicts, soldiers who have made war on civilians haven't just destroyed property, as Sherman had. They have tortured and killed innocent people. Sherman would have been horrified to think that his actions might have led to theirs.

The legacy that would have made him proudest was that, next to Grant, he was the general most responsible for preserving the Union. Sherman was an imperfect general. He never won a major battle, but he may have been the most brilliant American military man ever when it came to organizing a campaign. Sherman also understood that there were qualities in a general that were far more important than flash and dash.

"The true way to be popular with troops is not to be free and familiar with them, but to make them believe you know more than they do," Sherman once said. "My men believe I know everything; they are much mistaken but it gives them confidence in me."

Timeline

1820	William Tecumseh Sherman is born in Lancaster, Ohio, on February 8.
1829	Sherman's father dies. Sherman moves in with the family of Thomas Ewing.
1836	Sherman enters the U.S. Military Academy at West Point.
1840	Sherman graduates from West Point and is stationed at Fort Pierce, in Florida.
1842	Sherman is assigned to Fort Moultrie, in Charleston, South Carolina.
1846	The United States declares war on Mexico. Sherman is sent to Pittsburgh and then to California.
1850	Sherman marries Ellen Ewing.
1852	Sherman is transferred to New Orleans.
1853	Sherman resigns from the army. He becomes the business manager at the Lucas & Turner bank in San Francisco.
1857	Sherman moves to New York to set up a Lucas & Turner bank there.
1859	Sherman becomes superintendent of the Louisiana Seminary of Learning and Military Academy.
1860	South Carolina secedes from the Union.
1861	Sherman resigns from the seminary.
	The Civil War begins.
	Sherman returns to the army and participates in the Battle of Bull Run. He is promoted to brigadier general.

1862   Sherman distinguishes himself in the Battle of Shiloh.

1863   The Union wins the Battle of Vicksburg.

Sherman drives the Confederate general Joseph Johnston out of Mississippi.

1864   Sherman is named commanding general in the West. He takes control of Atlanta.

Sherman leads the March to the Sea, marching his men from Atlanta to Savannah.

1865   Sherman's men march through South Carolina and North Carolina.

Lee surrenders to Grant.

Johnston surrenders to Sherman.

1869   Sherman becomes commanding general of the army.

1884   Sherman retires from the army.

Sherman refuses the Republican nomination for president.

1891   William Tecumseh Sherman dies in New York on February 14.

Glossary

alienating: (AY-lee-uh-nayt-ing) Something that causes someone to feel hostile or unfriendly, when before one felt pleasant or good humored.

annexation (a-nek-SAY-shun) The adding of one piece of territory to another, as the United States annexed Texas in 1845.

assess (uh-SES) To determine the value, the importance, or the size of something.

arsenal (AR-sih-nul) A storehouse of weapons.

baptize (BAP-tyz) To sprinkle someone with or to immerse someone in water to show that person's acceptance into the Christian faith.

bayonets (bay-oh-NETS) Knives attached to the front ends of rifles.

Bill of Rights (BIL UV RYTS) The first ten amendments to the U.S. Constitution.

brutal (BROO-tul) Harsh, unfeeling, inhuman.

casualties (KA-zhul-teez) The number of soldiers killed, wounded, or captured in battle.

cavalry (KA-vul-ree) The part of an army that rides and fights on horseback.

civilian (sih-VIL-yin) A person who is not in the military.

commissary (KAH-mih-sayr-ee) A supermarket for military workers and their families.

Confederacy (kun-FEH-duh-reh-see) The eleven southern states that declared themselves separate from the United States in 1860 and 1861.

contradictions (kon-truh-DIK-shunz) Acts of saying the opposite of, disagreeing, or having a different opinion.

corruption (kuh-RUP-shun) Dishonesty; a departure from what is right.

demerits (dih-MER-its) Marks on a person's record that will count against him or her in the future.

devout (dih-VOWT) Very religious.

forage (FOR-ij) To hunt or search for something.

furlough (FUR-loh) A vacation for a soldier.

garrison (GAR-ih-sun) A military post.

implementing (IM-pluh-ment-ing) To carry out, or to fulfill an order, or an action.

ingeniously (in-JEEN-yus-lee) Doing something with cleverness, skill, or originality.

infantry (IN-fun-tree) The part of an army that fights on foot.

leave of absence (LEEV UV AB-sens) Time off from a job without pay.

legacy (LEH-guh-see) Something left behind by a person's actions.

line (LYN) A military arrangement in battle in which soldiers are placed next to one another in a line. If there is a break in the line, the enemy can get behind some of the soldiers and inflict horrible damage.

militia (muh-LIH-shuh) A group of volunteer or citizen soldiers who are organized to assemble in emergencies.

Northwest Ordinance (NORTH-west OR-dih-nens) The 1787 law that established how the territory north of the Ohio River would be governed and how sections of this territory would be able to apply for admission to the Union as states.

pallbearer (PAHL-behr-er) A person who helps to carry the coffin at a funeral.

plantation (plan-TAY-shun) A very large farm. During the 1700s and the 1800s, many plantation owners used slaves to work on these farms.

raise a regiment (RAYZ UH REH-jih-ment) To sign up enough volunteer soldiers to fill a regiment, or a large group of soldiers.

Reconstruction (ree-kun-STRUK-shun) A period in U.S. history after the Civil War (1865–1877) when the Confederate states attempted to rebuild their economies.

recruit (ree-KROOT) To sign up new soldiers for the military.

reinforcements (ree-in-FORS-ments) Anything that strengthens, specifically additional troops or warships to make stronger those already sent.

relieved of his command (rih-LEEVD UV HIZ kuh-MAND) Taken out of charge of a military unit.

secede (sih-SEED) To withdraw from a group or a country.

siege (SEEJ) Blocking off a fort or city with soldiers so that nothing can get in or go out.

skirmish (SKUR-mish) A brief fight or encounter.

smoke screen (SMOHK SKREEN) Something that is designed to confuse or disguise an issue or a thing.

strategy (STRA-tuh-jee) The science of planning and directing large military movements.

tactics (TAK-tiks) Maneuvering forces into the best position before and during a battle.

Union (YOON-yun) Another name for the United States before the Civil War. During the Civil War, it became the name of the Northern and border states that did not secede.

vagabonds (va-guh-BONDZ) People who wander from place to place without a destination.

veterans (VEH-tuh-runz) People who have fought in a war.

vindictive (vin-DIK-tiv) Someone who is seeking revenge, who purposely tries to be hurtful.

volunteers (vah-lun-TEERZ) Soldiers who had jobs outside the military before choosing to enlist in the army.

Additional Resources

If you would like to learn more about William Tecumseh Sherman, check out the following books and Web sites:

Books

Blassingame, Wyatt. *William Tecumseh Sherman: Defender of the Union*. Englewood Cliffs, N.J.: Prentice-Hall, Inc., 1970.

Clinton, Catherine. *Scholastic Encyclopedia of the Civil War*. New York: Scholastic Reference, 1999.

Hakim, Joy. *War, Terrible War*. New York: Oxford University Press, 1999.

Ray, Delia. *Behind the Blue and Gray: The Soldier's Life in the Civil War*. New York: Oxford University Press, 1999.

Sandler, Martin W. *Civil War*. New York: HarperCollins Publishers, 1996.

Web Sites

Due to the changing nature of Internet links, PowerPlus Books has developed an online list of Web sites related to the subject of this book. This site is updated regularly. Please use this link to access the list: www.powerkidslinks.com/lalt/sherman/

Bibliography

American National Biography. Vols. 9, 21, 23. New York: Oxford University Press, 1999.

Catton, Bruce. *U. S. Grant and the American Military Tradition*. New York: Grosset & Dunlap, 1954.

Hirshson, Stanley P. *The White Tecumseh: A Biography of General William T. Sherman*. New York: John Wiley & Sons, 1997.

Lewis, Lloyd. *Sherman: Fighting Prophet*. New York: Harcourt, Brace and Co., 1932.

Long, E. B., with Barbara Long. *The Civil War Day by Day: An Almanac 1861–1865*. Garden City, N.Y.: Doubleday, 1971.

Marszalek, John F. *Sherman: A Soldier's Passion for Order*. New York: Vintage Books, 1993.

Sherman, John. *Recollections of Forty Years in the House, Senate, and Cabinet: An Autobiography*. Chicago: The Werner Co., 1895.

Sherman, William Tecumseh. *Memoirs of General W. T. Sherman*. Notes by Charles Royster. New York: Library of America, 1990.

Simpson, Brooks D., and Jean V. Berlin, eds. *Sherman's Civil War: Selected Correspondence of William T. Sherman, 1860–1865*. Chapel Hill, N.C.: The University of North Carolina Press, 1999.

Index

About the Author

Lynn Hoogenboom has written biographical articles for *Dictionary of American Biography, American National Biography*, and *Scribner American Biography*. She has worked for three wire services and is currently the weekend editor at the New York Times News Service. She has a longstanding interest in the Civil War in general and in William Tecumseh Sherman in particular.

About the Consultant

John Dye is a practicing architect and an amateur Civil War historian. He lives in Lancaster, Ohio, the hometown of General Sherman. He is a former president of the Fairfield Heritage Association, which maintains Sherman's home as a museum.

Primary Sources

Cover. *William Tecumseh Sherman*, photo, ca. 1860s, Mathew Brady, Library of Congress Prints and Photographs Division. Background, *Battle of Shiloh*, painting, ca. 1888, Thure de Thulstrup, Library of Congress Prints and Photographs Division. **Page 4.** *W. T. Sherman*, photo, ca. 1863, J.P Greenwald and L. Longhorst, Schoff Civil War Collections, William L. Clements Library, University of Michigan. **Page 12.** *Thomas Ewing*, oil on canvas, William G. Browne, 1879, US Dept. Of Treasury. **Page 15.** *West Point*, lithograph created from oil painting, George Catlin, 1828, The Phelps Stokes Collection, Miriam and Ira D. Wallach Division of Arts, Prints and Photographs, New York Public Library, Astor, Lenox, and Tilden Foundations. **Page 16.** *Manual of military pyrotechny for the use of the cadets of the U.S. Military Academy*, West Point, title page, 1831, Science, Industry and Business Library, New York Public Library Astor, Lenox, and Tilden Foundations. **Page 20.** *Fort Moultrie, Charleston Harbor*, black ink and watercolor on tan paper, A. Vizitelly, 1861, Library of Congress Prints and Photographs Division. **Page 21.** *City of Charleston, South Carolina, looking across Cooper's River*, engraving and aquatint with watercolor, ca. 1838, G. Cooke, W.J. Bennett, Library of Congress Prints and Photographs Division. **Page 22.** *Mrs. William Tecumseh Sherman*, oil on canvas, 1868, George Peter Alexander Healy, Smithsonian American Art Museum, Washington, DC, U.S.A. **Page 25.** The harbor at Rio de Janeiro, sketch, 1847, W.T. Sherman, Archives of University of Notre Dame. **Page 28.** *Henry Clay*, daguerreotype, ca. 1850s, Mathew Brady, Library of Congress Prints and Photographs Division. **Page 32.** Sherman's home, sketch on the back of a bank check, 1855, W.T. Sherman, Archives of University of Notre Dame. **Page 36.** Sherman as superintendent of the Louisiana Seminary of Learning and Military Academy, oil painting, 1860, Louisiana State University Archives. **Page 41.** *Colonel Burnside's Brigade at Bull Run*, drawing on green paper with pencil, Chinese white, and black in wash, 1861, Alfred Waud, Library of Congress Prints and Photographs Division. **Page 44.** *Bacon's Military Map of the United States*, 1862, Library of Congress Geography and Map Division. **Page 45.** *Simon Cameron*, photo, ca. 1860s, Library of Congress Prints and Photographs Division. **Page 47.** *Major General Henry W. Halleck*, photo, ca. 1860s, J.A. Scholten, Library of Congress Prints and Photographs Division. **Page 50.** *Battle of Shiloh* Thure de Thulstrup, painting, ca. 1888, Library of Congress Prints and Photographs Division. **Page 53.** Sketch of a dead horse, graphite on paper, ca. 1860s, Alfred Waud, Library of Congress. **Page 58-59.** Panoramic view of the Vicksburg National Military Park and Vicinity, painting, ca. 1925, Poole Brothers, Chicago, Library of Congress Geography and Map Division. **Page 60.** *Joseph Eggleston Johnston*, oil on board, Benjamin Franklin Reinhart, National Portrait Gallery, Smithsonian Institution. **Page 62.** *W.T. Sherman*, photo, ca. 1860s, Mathew Brady, Library of Congress Prints and Photographs Division. **Page 63.** Army of the Cumberland Roll of Honor, certificate for veterans of the Army of the Cumberland, ca.1883, Middleton, Strobridge & Co., Lithographers, Library of Congress Prints and Photographs Division. **Page 66.** *General Sherman & Staff Passing Over the Pontoon Bridge*, graphite on paper, 1864, William Waud, Library of Congress Prints and Photographs Division. **Page 70.** Map illustrating the Siege of Atlanta, Ga. by the U.S. forces, created from an original map by Captain O.M. Poe, Corps of Engineers, lithograph, 1866, O.M. Poe, Library of Congress Geography and Map Division. **Page 72.** *W.T. Sherman on Horseback at Federal Fort No. 7.*, photo, 1864, George Barnard, Library of Congress Prints and Photographs Division. **Page 75.** Atlanta, Georgia, after the fire, photo, ca. 1864, George Barnard, National Archives and Records Administration. **Page 78.** Union foraging party on a Georgia farm, engraving, 1888, James E. Taylor and R.A. Muller. **Page 82-83.** *Columbia the Morning After the Fire*, drawing on orange paper with pencil, Chinese white and black ink wash, 1865, William Waud, Library of Congress Prints and Photographs Division. **Page 85.** *The Peacemakers*, oil on canvas, 1868, George Healy, White House Collection, White House Historical Association. **Page 88.** The Grand Review of the great armies of Grant, Sherman at Washington, on the 23rd and 24th May, 1865, photo, 1865, E. & H.T. Anthony, Library of Congress Prints and Photographs Division. **Page 93.** *W.T. Sherman*, photo, 1880s, Archives of the University of Notre Dame. **Page 95.** Union Veterans of the Civil War, including W.T. Sherman, photo, ca. 1884, Library of Congress Prints and Photographs Division.

Credits

Photo Credits

Cover, back cover, pp. 20, 21, 28, 41, 45, 47, 50, 53, 62, 63, 66, 72, 82–83, 88, 95 Library of Congress Prints and Photographs Division; p. 4 Schoff Civil War Collections, William L. Clements Library; p. 8 © The Field Museum, #A93851c, Photographer Ron Testa; p. 11 Ohio Historical Society Archives/Library; p. 12 courtesy of the Treasury Department; p. 15 the Phelps Stokes Collection, Miriam and Ira D. Wallach Division of Art, Prints, and Photographs, New York Public Library Astor, Lenox and Tilden Foundations; p. 16 courtesy of the Science, Industry, and Business Library, New York Public Library Astor, Lenox, and Tilden Foundations; p. 22 Smithsonian American Art Museum, Washington, D.C./Art Resource, NY; pp. 25, 31, 32, 64, 91, 92, 93 Archives of the University of Notre Dame; p. 26 courtesy Palmquist Collection; p. 35 LSU Photography Collection, RG# A5000, Louisiana State University Archives, LSU Libraries, Baton Rogue; p. 36 LSU Photography Collection, Louisiana State University Archives, LSU Libraries, Baton Rogue; pp. 44, 58–59, 70 Library of Congress Geography and Map Division; p. 60 National Portrait Gallery, Smithsonian Institution/Art Resource, NY; p. 75 National Archives and Records Administration, #NWDNS-165-SC-46; p. 78 The Irma and Paul Milstein Division of United States History, Local History, and Genealogy, New York Public Library Astor, Lenox, and Tilden Foundations; p. 79 Chicago Historical Society; p. 85 White House Collection, White House Historical Association; p. 97 The Rosen Publishing Group, photo by Patrick Henry Horran.

Project Editor
Daryl Heller

Series Design
Laura Murawski

Layout Design
Corinne L. Jacob

Photo Researcher
Jeffrey Wendt